HOW DO I LOVE TO FLY WITH MY SEX ?

HOW DO I LOVE TO FLY WITH MY SEX ?

Sakshi Vasudev

KALPAZ

ISBN: 978-81-7835-964-9

Price: ₹180

First Published 2013

Published by

Kalpaz Publications
C-30, Satyawati Nagar,
Delhi - 110052
E-mail: kalpaz@hotmail.com Ph.: 9212142040

Laser Typesetting: Rajender Vashist, Delhi
Printed at: G. Print Process, Delhi

Cataloging in Publication Data--DK
Courtesy: D.K. Agencies (P) Ltd. <docinfo@dkagencies.com>

Sakshi Vasudev.
How do I love to fly with my sex? / Sakshi Vasudev.
p. cm.
Novel.
ISBN 9788178359649

1. Sex--Fiction. 2. Indic fiction (English). I. Title.

DDC 823.92 23

Dedication

I feel I have everything when I am with you
I feel blessed when you swap it crimson from blue
I feel I should dedicate this to the one we all love
I feel He holds the credit more than I do

Acknowledgement

My acknowledgement is genuine, factual and flaxen.

To all,

Those who say me no, Let me know!!

This would actually have not been possible without "ALL".

Foremost approbation to a sincere friend – SAMY. The first step had been taken along, trusting a mere stranger-HE, who but never behaved bizarrely.

I would express my deep gratitude to TINU, a dearest friend, for his patient guidance, enthusiastic encouragement and useful critiques which escorted thus my dream work. His willingness to give his time so generously has been very much appreciated.

I would extend my thanks to the Kalpaz Publications for their help in offering me the resources in running the programme. I had to be grateful too to the staff of the said company in particular, for being a part and parcel in the making of this dream come true.

Special thanks to the silent but wobbly characters of my story.

Sakshi Vasudev

Preface

Writing this book had not been worth, without sharing of her, his learned acumen:

Sex is important

Age never hinders us to find one to love – 17's to 60's all have a love story that somehow ended or has just begun. It always plays pendulum between happy or sad ending. Reason, absence of love – the betrayal or the presence of love – the union.

Love Never Do Hurt,
It's Always the Absence of Love that Does.

Had read Kamala Dass, a female writer, not ever guilty of her words – being criticised for sharing her life's sensual secrets.

David Levithan had been a male writer in lane, taking gay, the homosexual as the core for couple of his writings.

But had they not tried...

> I had been making an effort to nip this passion in the bud as I knew my pen would say lots more than I could ever emit out of my mouth. It was high time writing in my daily dairy, facebook walls – the most loved and hated experiences of life, thus exploiting my writing credentials to the limits.

To compile it in a book, it's a little effort put to indulge you all. As it's a story where you will find yourself playing an untold, unsaid and unexplained role. My words and your play – sharing my experience with millions there in the world experiencing the same – a first sight love, a breakup, a patch up, a new relation, or something that may never be named too.

I was growing old to follow traditions of getting married in twenties; I had to dare and come out shaking shackles of reality to let my dreams come true. I had to see myself as a contended, cherished and successful writer. Success needs you do something first or do what has never been done before – sitting quiet does not let a miracle happen, as even the still water stinks. Your participation as a reader makes this role play a triumph.

More confidence comes when you trust the most worthy person. The one who never tells a lie, never let your expectations come down. One who does not demand you to hide the truth. One who knows what you really want to have – SELF. Being alone really helped me in making the utmost of this.

Need to remember that every ending itself says – it's time to begin though again.

Cited – "For trust not him that hath once broken faith"
—William Shakespeare, *King Henry VI, Part 3*

World's most optimistic inventions are a helping aid when shared. I too wish, every reader has lips widened as they finish reading the closing sentence of the last page of my first book. Let me invite you all for this loyal, sensual, love filled journey of pondering tears to glittery smiles, exposing ...

SEX IS ...... !!!!!

Sakshi Vasudev

I have always found a similitude between books and women. Both of these have many things to say – but hardly do say. Just letting others understand!!!

Unlike others – I've let them speak, whatever they want.

It is not every girl, woman, lady who wants to, but sake of being the same to men never let them do so.

It's the story of not an individual but many who had been living, leaving the same life.

It's not the story of betrayal and love.

It is the story of a virgin slut – proving she was never born but made to live like one, by none other than her own lover.

Prologue

Seeing this, I would sense coyness. I preferred closing eyes to perceive it more vigilant. We had a sensual bond, that binds me to him. He had his warmth around my bust. As we went more cozy, I fell a prey to his love. I hadn't hesitated knowing he wanted me to love him, too. I indulged in my first love making thus.

"Love you", I oozed.

"Love you, too", he sighed.

As my bosom did welcome his masculine touch, I gave him a comfy push, though I didn't mean it. He clinched my fists firmly to bring me closer. My heart pumped blood a thousand times more than regular. Our lips went seducing us to prolong this moment. We closed our eyes again. A gentle touch explored my eyes, ears, neck and deep of it. I couldn't move an inch. The world around had blocked all hindering. It formed a sphere within Adam and Eve left alone.

"I want to love you like there is no tomorrow", he said.

A sensation ran down my nerves meeting his eyes. No luxuries in the world are worth fetching the comfort, your beloved's embrace does. Audible sighs of this passion was the best music now.

"Gudia! Gudia! Gudia !" He jolted me hard.

Yes, I was more than baffled at this open eyed dream.

Wow ! It was wonderful to be your heroine again, I thought.

"What..? What are you saying, Gudia? I hope you are fine".

I went closer to hug him again, a cute smile widened my lips. "I am always good when with you", I said.

"Hmmmmm.." and otherwise you remain contrary, he asked.

"Ha ! Ha ! yes, else you will say I am not like you" bad.

He could not help laughing now.

I ogle, his chinky eyes had a casting spell. I love this since I met him. He told me once that government should impose penalty on him for smiling this way. It could harm him and others, driving with eyes closed.

I grumbled when the car whisked to take us away from this love land. I longed to be with him for at least this span of life. But now it was the time for girls to do justice to the traditional values learned. I had to be home by now.

Dropping me in front of my home, he was poignant.

"I wish if we could spend some more time together", he whispered.

I wonder if he read minds. Shall I join him again? But soon curbed this oddity.

"Hey, cheer up ! I am still alive", I said.

He smiled. "Really, I thought you are dying this very night", he cracked a joke.

"For you I will keep my words, darling, stay ready for the ghost night", I sniggered.

"Ha ! Ha! Now go and love you mad girl", he said.

"Same to you", I said and winked at him.

Was it for love, or...? he asked.

You know me, no...? and I ran.

Wait ! I will tell you better, he leaned to seize me before my exit from car.

But I had a lucky escape. I waved him goodbye. A flying kiss was all he could get.

Love to drape his smile.

I moved lethargically. But I was seeing him the next day, too. I consoled my poor heart somehow.

"Reached safely?" I messaged him.

"Reached safely, love you. Meeting tomorrow?"

"Love you, too. Yes, anything for you. Good night love."

Good night, muahhh.

"Muaaah 2, thanks." Message sent, shyness beamed more than the light of cellphone in dark room.

I switched off every light to ensure I could be at rest. I tried but had him sitting next to me and his hold unsullied. I need to shut my eyes to this reality to welcome him in my dreamland, too.

And now after an year. . .

That night's memories were haunting this night. It was leading to dawn. I hadn't had a nap. I was again chatting. It was of reunion. Though every day I wait to love him, to be loved. But knowing it was his timepass, he was alone, that's why. He didn't love instead he had fucked me, his wife that night.

Prologue 2

Bad dream......! Thank God. Sweating, I woke up as if I had a cardiac arrest. Since she told me her story, I hadn't even had a wink of sleep at night. Now her tale had my head as its permanent domicile. Her name was Gudia. As she was named, so were her deeds. All befooled her. Now, her story had befooled my sleep. When the night couldn't put me to bed, I woke up and lit every light. I had my laptop on my stage and my fingers running on its keys. This nearly dead story demands creation through my words.

Why to rape when the paid hostesses are accessible? Why sex is considered important? Why all women are not alike? What makes love and lust differ? What is true love? Why the capable feels handicaped to stick to certain decisions? Are sluts ever born or made? Why love stories? Why more trust ends in mistrust? Why uncountable reasons for smile bring woes, too? Why the one we once loved, starts haunting with its presence in life? What induces one to commit suicide? What is truly fake – orthodox or ultra modern?

Though I had kept mum, when she asked. But now I had the answers out of her utterance.

Sometimes mere answers don't serve the purpose. Pre-requisite now was to find a solution. If most of the wives compromise. It was not marriage. Gudia had not been the culprit but a victim to the cruel beings around. She had suppressed her elevated voice. For her every boring trend could be exploited with one's perception. Weird the ways to such thinking as she herself had no perception. All she knew was to care the one's she was in love with. All she hated was nothing but hatred. She could make one laugh with her pranks. Now she was not laughed at by herself even. I remember how she seated herself opposite to me to play the flashback. I had known her by her cute yet pale face. Her words made me familiar, she was a woman. She got the clinch of my attention starting. . . .

Sex is Important – he taught me this.

Chapter 1

"Every tear attests worth a smile"

'Red is the best colour that suits me', she planted a kiss on the mirror. The impression of her lips painted in red lip colour looked seducing. She was talking to herself. She was her favourite.

Enough for today, she said. If someone comes I will be beaten to red, too.

Hearing the footsteps, she rubbed palm on her lips but it tinted her chubby cheeks, too.

A slap added more charm to her beauty. She turned a silent but wobbly rose. "What are you doing here with all this?" her aunt screamed.

"Nothing", she scowled with all her innocence. She had nothing more to say. To flee was the best she did.

This had gone the regular practice now but her love for red color remained alike. She stood sobbing. As she glanced the world around, the beverage container grabbed her attention. While all were served the soft drink, she had to quench her thirst merely by watching. But now, she had not waited another second to gulp its sip. As it ran down her throat, she chucked. Her heart sank. It was not coke but phenyl. She ran to emit it out. But had inhaled it to an extent and felt giddy. The next moment she landed.

She woke up in her bed with puffy eyes. Her head still playing pendulum. She was in oblivion.

'Do you need more coke?' She was being mocked at by the spectators.

She filled her eyes with tears. Mob hadn't consoled her with a warm hug. Even the parent toiled cold.

A child could not help self more than shedding tears in solitude. She did that while driving the punctured cycle passed on to her, which was announced of no use. She saw her face in side mirror. She smiled in tears.

It was red.

'Getting angry is to punish self for the mistake of others'.

Chapter 2

"When the world walks out, Only Hope whispers,

Try it one more time".

The principal episode haunted her mind. The art of making money is important, she realised. But more cruel were the ways to find that only 'Money makes the mare go'.

"May I come in, sir"? she almost pleaded.

"Wait, no need to come in", the principal replied.

He had simply denied her entry in the classroom. He had turned down her request for the continuation of studies for a fee remission. Now all she could do was to request him again. Into the extreme depths her heart sank. Confined to the core, she loved her books. The bell rang drawing her to face him for the last time.

"Ask your father if he can come to see me", the principal said. "I have bunch of jobs for him". He left the classroom cleaving the application.

That evening, after school, she felt pissed off. It reminded her of his curt reply. But somehow, she assembled enough courage to discuss the matter with her father. What should I tell him? If he will come to know that I had begged of him for a fee concession, I will be dead. She kept her little mind at work with hodge-podge of all the odds and evens.

"Stay at home then. Who will pay huge sum every month?" I can't. His father said firmly.

"Why..? I have to study. You need to pay just a visit. Sir will do the rest, dad, he has promised." Gudia said earnestly.

He left the room, irritated.

'Only the fortunate do study and the rest stay otherwise', was her eloquence.

In life there is everything one can do, but will to do makes the difference. She strangulated dreams of expecting any waiver either from him or him. Both him's denoted men, a father, a principal.

> *"We do understand, who understands us after us. It's most of the time God, but sometimes, God in His human form too."*

Another day at school.

"Who is Gudia?" one of the maids had come to inquire.

Completely perplexed, Gudia had raised her hand.

"Your parents are at the reception", maid said.

My eyes glazed in the dimly lit classroom. But who would have favour paying my fee, she thought. She rapidly paced to detect.

At the reception, few of the students from junior wing were crying to go back home with their parents. It was tough to invent the meaning out of their language.

The Mango was *mando*, Class was *tlass* for them.

Few of the sick ones were pretending artlessly. Seeing the teachers around, one of them coughed breathlessly. It was phony. Even I did once the same way, I cackled.

It took me fifteen minutes to ensure that my parents were not there. I was to ask the maid. But heard someone calling my name, Gudia.

I turned to find one of my friends and her family.

'Hi Saj, *Namaste* aunty', paying my regards. I joined them.

Her mother lugged me in her lap. I struggled to set free. "We paid the dues. Your books are here. Take this pen and show your credentials. I will pay for you. But you have to promise the continuation of studies. I have three daughters. Will you please join them..?", her mother said.

It moistened my eyes. I hugged her, this was the best comfort I had had since birth. It was love, sanctified.

Gudia folded hands to thank God. Squeezing her cherry nose she smiled.

"When you are able to see even when eyes closed

Is your God you have met."

I gained what I had lost once, self-confidence.

***

"God was what was good in me, I had eradicated evils since ages"

The revolution had the English literature introduced in school. Though the teacher himself unaware, taught us. This subject remained orphan until we pressurised school authorities to adopt it for us. While I opted literature, Saj was left behind with her vocational subjects. We hardly met but the trend to pay in advance continued. Given a chance, we coupled. It was more than a lottery by His grace but to study.

While others stick to tutions, Gudia skilled her brains.

Saj disregarded the credit. She never asked for it even. Money never belongs to happiness, Saj said.

Saj had heaps of it. What makes her say so? Gudia wondered.

Gudia had asked her that rebirth will only repay this all. "As she is not that able now. What if it happens?"

"If I say, I am returning it to you, you had lent this to me in previous birth", Saj answered.

Saj was humble and had passed on her trait to my nerves. Eating an extra meal sounds abrupt but sharing a fraction with the hungry bird was a more idyllic thing. She did this. She had been aware of the worth riches carry.

Only the millionaire on his death bed can explain the best. "Pay attention to your studies. I had not lent you a loan", Saj concluded.

More than mere notes, Gudia had love and care from them, without toiling for it. She had not dreamt of visiting such places. Saj paid for most of the school trips.

In life one may have friends. But one who is more than friend is a blessing in disguise. A girl was helping, family had no say for this. Not even once they troubled to ask me anything.

The same place, from where I was sent back home when fee unpaid, had now witnessed me receiving award for the best student of school for the session. My school dress had many of the tattered sewed. Where others botched, I succeeded. I was proud of myself.

The real struggle awaited me at the threshold. It marked my exit from school as a topper for the year. Entering the span of College, dreams of staying topper was the only treasure I had.

The girl earlier not aware of her today, could see her tomorrow with an ease now.

Chapter 3

"O Lord ! I Pray thee ! I Praise thee !
Shall we have the mercy ! Shall we have the care!
We With your Grace once did and will do dare".

The huge building of college, and city roads I had never been to. Crowd equivalent to the mob of students at school for morning prayers. A big library will proffer more to read. I was excited.

Another challenge, I wanted all of them to know me.

It was miracle, when a schoolmate had asked me to accompany her to college for admission. Fortunate I was to manage enough funds for the documents required. Unfortunate was that girl, I invaded her because of my good percentage. It was like her help had me in college. It was destined. But I had massaged heels to make it happen. Government had the strict procedures for attestation and all. Later I found Nama, a good friend from my previous school, in college. Though we hailed from middle class, we had decided to save more for study materials. Dividing time to walk on foot for this. I had coupons for refreshment from NCC, thus both of us managed to have cup of tea only during winters. We had always managed to buy books for ourselves. All we had in mind was to learn somehow. We had commuted our problems. We had nothing left under shade for each other.

Even Saj couldn't make up for her admission in this renowned and reputed college of the town as she couldn't match high scores as required. She passed me a packet. "Pay your fee. My fate is for another institution", she said.

"I will study with same zeal", I said.

She hugged me. "You need anything. Call me, have my number?"

"Yes, I am having. Thanks Saj", I said holding her hands.

"No thanks, you are always welcome. You always smile. But it is your veil to tears, I know. You have the most naive smile in this world. I want to hoard this for you."

Gudia bid her farewell, her eyes thanked Saj. She left her with goose bumps.

First day in College.

The journey initiated. Being elected the class representative was the best start. Auditorium was bashed. Next, it was my turn during elections for the same.

I ascended stage, while others had promised sham.

I closed my eyes chanting...

Eh zindagi paani diyan chaar challan

Ehna challan ne pata ni kado sukk jana

Hass khed ke zindagi guzar layiye

Ehna sahan ne pata ni kado mukk jana

Ehna sahan ne...

Hooting and prompting followed as the poll head announced my name.

Holder of highest votes, Gudia is our next representative. Others had only one or two votes to their credit.

'Love you all', I thanked them.

'Love you, too', the mob shouted in unison.

It all ended when I left college as Republic Day Parade attendant, my poetry honoured by Surjit Patar, Best cadet for Ludhiana and 2nd best for Punjab. I won to be the best dressed for the year.

I would not have this, unless I owned this sex.

Chapter 4

"A little knowledge is not dangerous for those who seek more knowledge out of little one".

The atmosphere was not casual but more tensed. I was at NCC Headquarters. Here only phoenix survive, no room for fragile. The posters posed elegant cadets with notable personalities.

I, too, will join them, was my soliloquy. We went conscientious as our Col. arrived. We saluted to respect his rank.

"Sir, can she be our next BC", our NCC ANO (officer) requested. "She is talented. She sings and dances well. She is a public speaker. She is well-built. She is confident", my ANO continued excitedly.

"I can't say anything unless I test her", his looks stern.

His words hobbled in Gudia's mind. "I am General, not backward caste, what is she talking about? Gudia was talking to herself and his voice perturbed her self-indulgence.

"What is your name?" he asked.

"Yes, pardon", I went attentive.

"Gudia, Gudia J is my name", sir. I replied.

"What are your hobbies?", he probed.

Singing, dancing, speaking, reading and writing, was all I had to say.

"What do you write?" he asked.

"What others don't dare to", I answered deliberately.

"That's confidence! good." he said.

"Which all dances you know", he proceeded to inquire more.

"Any of the dances, I can learn. I love learning almost everything", I replied..

"What if I train you for next Best Cadet Competition? You will have tough life waking up at 4 am and ending at the last hours of the day. Sometimes it may deprive you of your sleep and food, too. You will be trained for firing, swimming, public speaking, horse riding, dancing, singing and acting. Your writing skills may help you too. But you will have to win this for us. Interested..?"

A little knowledge is really a dangerous thing. Now the backward caste was best cadet. Else she would have relinquished this opportunity. She smiled.

"Yes, I am", Gudia replied confidently.

"Enroll her, she is good", he told my ANO as we were to leave.

Gudia made self proud of what she did.

Dressed in army combat, I was all proud. People were staring in sheer surprise. I hired an auto rickshaw and the driver saluted. On my way, I had dreamt of firing the illicit. Auto jogged towards the destination.

"First day and you are late by five minutes. On your knees." She could not understand this. The Instructor was fuming at Gudia.

But I was breathless after five runs of the track. I was summoned for firing when I was nearly comatose. For the first time in my life, I clutched the rifle. It was a big one.

The instructor guided me. First few fires missed the target.

"Your fire is aiming right. Hold the rifle straight and firm", instructor scolded Gudia.

We halted the process as our Col. came into sight.

He guided Gudia the best way out of his experiences. Gudia looked at Col. again. He was middle aged with grey whiskers. He was well dressed and his personality poised.

Gudia's next target had all the bullets fired. She was happy.

"The best firer should stick to practice", Col told her.

They ended the beautiful day before lunch.

"Judging the books by its covers,

forged verdict".

"Good afternoon sir", Gudia greeted him with a smile. She was in NCC headquarters for the daily dose of English speaking.

"Good afternoon Gudia, Any progress? Show me the advancement card."

"Here it is", she handed him the target paper of firing.

"Wow ! your wisdom is in prime, I must say. This is going good."

"Thanks sir", Gudia said.

A JCO (holder of a junior rank) came to inquire, "You asked for water, which one sir?"

"Especially Pure one", he said smiling at his stupid question.

It stressed Gudia's mind. Water is water. Stay alert, She directed self in eloquence. She was swayed by Bollywood movies where the culprit acts shrewd but pretends to be adorable.

She refused to drink it. He may have added something.

But the villain drank.

The next command pounded her. His message for camera petrified Gudia the most.

Examining the camera, he found it out of order. He shouted at his JCO. Government does not give us bundles of money. "Go and ask for replacement today only, our cadets are leaving for Singapore tonight. They will miss their camp memories without this gadget."

Seeing Gudia smile, 'you too will go for one of such camps, my child', he said.

Was he aware of the reason behind this smile, I was perplexed. I was relieved – he was not villain.

While preparing me for the interview, he behaved abruptly. He crossed the table to reach me at another corner. He placed his hand on my left arm, I was vibrating.

"Keep this arm shoulder above your elbow", he directed.

I stood up in haste.

"Be seated", he said.

"Yes, Yes, I will do that", Gudia replied in panic.

"Even the best way to uniform counts, learn these things, too", he said. "You smudge your triumph a sure".

Oh ! How brainless I was, Gudia thought. But it was all about learning out of stupid experiences.

I had failed to utter a single word in English on the first day of training. But now I sounded fluent. His strict rules were the reason behind. And of course, her brainless brain, too. Gudia smiled.

"Only practice doesn't make a man perfect, the will to practice do".

"You have made it through finals, My Best cadet", my Col. sir said proudly." "You are 1st best."

Yeahhhhhhh ! I was so happy. Sleepless nights had this reward. Of course, his criticism, too had been one of the reasons. For him, I could always do better. I hated it at times. But it had underneath, ensured my success.

"Better, if your parents come on your behalf" my Col. handed me the invitation for the prize distribution ceremony that was to be held on camp fire. You won't be able to come.You are chosen for next camp, too."

"Thanks sir", Gudia said happily.

She had cried with pain. Had relished the mud fights. Her friends had one or the other things to do but she had been the participant in every event. She had exploited her endurance.

Broke ankle during obstacle training. But to walk in the beautiful journey ahead was a must.

"You will have more of hurdles. Wish you good luck for this endeavor, my child", My Col. blessed me, placing his hand on my head.

It was best to feel the presence of absence, of a loved one, of a father.

Army truck cantered the roads of high grounds, Zirakhpur. The huge plane and plains both seemed hazardous. We were to reside in hangers. Either to worsen or to obscure the stay, the basic luxuries marked missing. Their life was in peril. Gudia along with other chosen cadets reached the site.

The same night, they had been assigned duties. Keeping the torch in hand and shove in head phones for music, they were night keepers. They named us *santris*. The fog around added more thrill. They were no more scared of dusk.

Junior Division (JD's) girls in temporary washrooms were hearing the droplet voices. They were betting whose shit will plunge first. Gudia laughed.

They had more of live comedy seeing one or the other running midway of junglepani in jungles at the sight of dogs and wolves. Sometimes keeping the comb and toothbrush in pocket. They had less time but they confer more.

Scarcity was the mother of all inventions. They invented means to tackle the punishment given for staying late for parade and firing. They had one dish plate and glass. They poured a jumble of all the dishes, keeping chapattis in pockets. Every day one was given the chance to enjoy the punishment to roll on floor with rifle for staying back to wash utensils. Others rushed to parade ground on allotted time.

One day a boy was caught red handed, he was smoking.

He argued, "I had never seen a cigarette".

The camp commandant picked one from behind his ear. "Its resting here, no..?" he mocked at him.

All giggled. Such chances never spared even friends.

It was fun.

Besides this, Gudia had no amusement left in life. She had to stay busy the big day. Her active participation had a reason for them to select her for the final camp held at Delhi. She had somehow managed a two hour sleep every night.

The day for pre-rehearsal came. She had been their first choice but she wished them to choose her. She was criticised and thrown out of group dance. She imitated their moves and proved that everything if willed can be learnt.

Finally Gudia boarded the bus along with other selected cadets. She was now lead dancer for the same group dance, she was not earlier even chosen for. They all had learned discipline. But they were more of the indisciplined. Their destination awaited to spin them civilised.

Their bus halted as they reached Parade Ground, Delhi. They were greeted the best way, drum beats thrilled them all. Seeing eatables, few lobbed luggage. They were sick of eating *aloo puris*. Pastries and patties lured. But they were to do as directed. The staff there was crook. They favour no favouritism. They had to be in line with rules.

She had chosen easily to come but to leave was toughest later on. It was hellish heaven.

At night, they were lined up for attendance and instructions. Seeing the fairy whites from Jammu and black skins from Tamil taught them, they were human first. Love conquered difference of caste, colour, creed, language, culture, states. Gudia befriended most of them. They were Indians.

Tomorrow at sharp 5 am, is that clear, our senior ANO. Camp was loud enough without a mike.

'Yes Mam', we all shouted in unison.

We had the tasty food and comfy beds after an year of filth and vermin. We slept as never to wake up.

'You all, wake up now', the way our ANO used to shout, Gudia smiled as if she was dreaming.

But the very next minute, they were out of their beds. It was the smoggiest morning. They were as sluggish as creepers.

Gudia and two of her friends, Gugu and Kittu intended to quit the hectic beginning. They rested outside the main gate holding rifles of friends too. Dense fog helped. They had joined the rest on their way back to the barrack. They were prank players and giggled shrewdly.

'Everyday I will be with you all for morning parades, understand', ANO (lady instructor in NCC) commanded with coarseness.

We could not help but laugh. 'Yes mam, we understand' was our reply.

A tall man guarded Director General (DG) residence. They were to salute passing the region. All chuckled seeing him smile as his moustaches widened. It denoted swing for kids, if wagged.

"The best and the worst things happened".

They grabbed the cultural best performance trophy. Many of the states and performers competed. Receiving the huge trophy had amplified trust in their credentials. It had complimented their dance performance too.

"Sir, can you please help me in holding this trophy", Gudia requested Col. as she was losing the grip. She was panting due to the much weighing trophy.

"Go and keep this in my office, he commanded. He hadn't heeded an inch to bother—

"I will sir, Gudia had to manage its deliverance to his office. It will be wrecked if lobbed".

"Stupid cadets, asking Col. to help them with trifles." he grumbled.

"Sorry Sir", she softened. Rich locks, Gudia mocked at him, picking up a long strand from his shoulder. She had passed him the trophy to relax her muscles.

He was baffled. "What"? he shouted. He went pale the next minute.

After a long pause, tension released. "It might be your. Your turban is veil to your locks, no..?" Gudia said.

Gudia mocked at him and escaped from the scene.

The best was to visit President, Prime Minister, Chief of Indian Army, Chief of Indian Navy, Chief of Air India. It was memorable seeing Dr. A.P.J. Abdul Kalam, escorted by so many of the guards coming at Rajpath. It made her dream come true. Defense minister A.K. Antony, Chief Minister Delhi Smt. Sheela Dixit and many of the dignitaries visited during our stay. She aired her views in front of them. Gudia was in the group of finest singers. They sang only patriotic songs for VIP visits. They had loved being Indians. Gudia had never attended the media interaction and was punched by her Col. for the same once.

Under the open sky, they had been attending parties. The buzzing flies tasted to help them choose which one of the dishes to relish first.

Love and hatred were in air "I love you bitch", one proposed Gudia.

"Fuck off", she replied.

"I want to fuck", he said.

"Charity begins at home, start with your sister first", she crooked.

It happened during her Delhi and Agra visit. He had approached Gudia with a plea to let him be her boyfriend. But she turned down his request. Later he went more of gay than a guy. Love was blind here all the time. Gudia made them see with their eyes but. She was famous. When few girls had come with a proposal too. She was arrogant moulding her attitude. After all, she was not to date girls.

Fortunately survived the unfortunate accident.

This bad thing happened in bus. Rakhi S, a stout girl, poured her sexy toned body on Gudia's backbone. Gudia came to know about it, when the very next day she could not move out of her bed. My friends consoled as if I had lost my soul. The stinking bodies and the sweating embrace had harassed me much. All friends were mothers. For the whole night, they were by my bedside. Gudia thanked the Army hospital who saved her from all this. It was taken as paralysis attack but in real it was not so. Gudia's friends dressed her in sari when she had a blissful return from the hospital.

Every night they used to steal eatables. Few girls were spared at night for sexy talks with their boyfriends. Gudia had witnessed a girl in her two piece. She was busy on phone.

Someone shouted, she looked hot. They had dragged her quilt down.

But Gudia could not even vomit seeing her in blue inners, awwwwwkkk.

That ugly seminude girl was shy, of what? We were rolling on floor.

Lesser time had made us more reprehensible. It was an ease to shed and change clothes in front of fellow friends but of the same sex alone.

We were given training of discipline. Now it was time for the fire fighting lessons but with a mere surprise.

Next evening, there was chaos all around. They followed the crowd. They were supposed to bring along the fire fighting equipments and had expected of a bomb blast at least. There was no fire. They were just trained to tackle, if it happens ever. But when it really broke down once, they ran holding the fire fighting equipments. The irony was not knowing its usage.

Flames were thrilling the adventurous beasts in them.

A lady officer was unable to hold her plump frame and slipped. She ran to save her life.

Gudia had an attitude and she loved it. The farewell day had its reception. Departure made them cry as they were not going to see anyone again. They managed enough CD's and photographs of friends and the competition to keep the memories alive. As Gudia had seen the Australian cadets standing under shade to smooch, she had no idea of doing the same one day, too, with none other than an Australian. It started the day she met one. . . .

Chapter 5

Choices do chaos, I choose.

She narrated it as........

Our story of love had its origin the day I witnessed a guy holding leather jacket in his hand on a social site. He was extra attentive of his looks. But he was as normal as any guy of his age would be. I was looking for one of my friends Meethu S, accidently met eyes with Meethu J. I had no idea to commune. Out of my rules, I did. It was strange to pass a sincere comment to a stranger.

"You look cute", I sent him a precise message.

"Thanks", came his reply.

The very next day, he was in my friends list. Among known, the stranger was more of known. I confessed, I was in love with him. He never knew until I spoke to him about it.When the perceptions clash, the arguments are born out. I told him that I was not a girl of his trade. I had no justification to offer. But I had to clear him of his doubts.

The sarcasm was, he had told me of my intentions, which he knew though I was not aware of.

"Girls long for NRI boys", he said.

"I don't think, if love is bounded by such conception". I almost yelled, "You don't deserve love". But the respect later dragged me to continue loving him. All I had for him was love. If I had trusted, I should stick to it. I can't let one hurt my self-respect. To free him of his qualms, insighted my perception.

Neither the presence nor the absence of a reason, when makes no difference, is love. I cited few of my readings and findings to define it.

"Didn't your mother love you before you were even born", I asked.

He was quiet.

A Sikh Professor in England was loved by one of the girl students of his child's age. A girl who was not afraid of a man in turban. She loved without expecting love in return. Prof. left England for his love for family, leaving her love behind. She cried but for what she never knew.

Another story engrosses an Orphan girl, Ratan, loving a postmaster. She was slipshod to relations. She was conscious of care, affection and passion, but not of love. The postmaster had no intentions for her. She fell in love with him somehow. Once the postmaster fell ill. She nursed him, fed him and cared for him. It always delighted her. But when he offered his salary against her pondering love, he was slapped. He was leaving, never to return. The saturation point was unlimited. He never cared for her and later was deprived of her love.

Live story of Prof. Matuknath went the only news media buzzed. He was in love with one of his students. But he had ditched his wife for the sensual pleasures.

When we do invite people to attend ceremonies, we never bother for class, creed, color, caste. But who perform rituals in ceremonies are confined to be our people. Love, if explained had no worth.

I told her how I had been in love with my Col. I owe him for what I am today. He earned my trust though as per others he was not meant for this trust. For the sake of others I do my sake.

Our chat ended.

He was pacified to the extent he could be. He had set enough fire to the sole base of my self-respect. He had asked me for my phone number, though half heartedly. I cried a lot. I was in the office that time. I told him to contact me later on. In the office, all were surprised to find me crying for no reason.

The phone beeped again as I sat sobbing in my cabin, I disconnected. Third time, I attended to his call after reaching home. For the very first time, I was hearing my gadget man.

I remained silent.

"Is this Ashi?", he asked.

I didn't answer.

"Are you there Ashi?", he asked again.

"Yes", I could hardly say. "I am here, say Mr. Meethu J, how are you?"

"I am good. Have you reached home safely?"

"Yes", I could not say more than this. His words had upset me. 'All girls need NRI's, I thought you are just flirting', I said. Men do trust less or sometimes don't. He did the same.

"What you think of yourself? If you don't trust, why did you rang?" I asked bluntly.

He was ashamed. He must have realised his folly of calling me a fool. Otherwise asking me for my cell number was his foolishness, too.

"Do you really need a reason", I asked

"No", he was silent.

"You are stupid", I said.

He smiled, "yes I am. How do you know?"

"I have seen your picture", I giggled.

"Oh ! Thanks for joining me." Miss stupid, he said laughing.

"Pleasure is entirely mine, good night", I said.

"Good night", Going home?"

"Why should I tell you", I stressed the last word.

"That's all right. goodbye", he went squat. "Don't cry more".

"Goodbye", I hung up the phone.

He was free to call me anytime. He had girls in his life. I was not as any of them. I could make him smile. I could shout at him. I could hug him and kiss him many times a day. I could listen to his worries. I could share his happiness, even if it was about his new undergarments.

"I had a pair of new ones, Jockey", he said.

I smiled..? "How are you?"

"I am happy in new ones", instant reply.

"Good, had food?" I left the topic in oblivion.

"Yes, else the fitting will go loose, if you will not care to feed me the best way."

Oh God ! I knew him. He will not switch over to another topic, without my say how.

"I too will buy the brand, fair name, no..?"

"What will you buy, uppers or lowers?" His next message.

"I will take you along", I giggled.

"Wow, will you let me in try-room?"

Mere illusion of escorted by him made me smile.

"Tell?" he asked again.

"You have gone insane. If you will not stop discussing it I will slap you hard". I replied.

"Is it so? I am dying for your touch baby. Where will you start from?"

"Meethu J You are crazy. I am not going to touch you".

"See, it doubles your happiness. You mean, I need to request you. I am here, please do the honour."

"May be Meethu J".

He replied in succession. "I want to keep listening to you".

"I wish you always smile with your chinky eyes. Love you", I said.

"Love you, too, *paharan*."

I never exchanged silly jokes but healthy humour.

I had chosen him to be mine. I had no reason to look for choices.

Chapter 6

"If you don't like the looks, you don't look to like."

My work place, A spa ambiance was a healing ground. It was noon. We had no clients for the day. I was roaming around in my office. I was drowsy after lunch. I went to *Jacuzzi* bath, I dipped my legs in water to relax. The soothing music formed its rhythm.

My phone vibrated and fell into the water.

I saw his number on screen. I plunged in the tub. My phone was dead. It was not well in diving and had drowned.

Alas ! I rushed to the nearby service centre to get my phone fixed.

"You will get it after two days, we need to change the screen", the representative said.

"WTF, I need it now man", I shouted.

"You should have taken care then", he was arrogant.

"I don't need your advice. Tell me the best you can do", I asked him.

"I can provide you another mobile model for the time being, it will cost you an additional rent for the same".

I agreed and came back to office, my Spa. I was angry at my folly of enjoying beach in tub. I sat to check my regular mails.

He was online.

I was in no mood to chat. I had my head roaring at myself.

"Hi!"

"Are you there?"

"Yes", I replied.

"I am home today" he said.

"Take rest then", I was in no mood to chat.

"How are you?" he asked.

"I didn't type but had sent smileys." ☺☺

"What happened?", he went serious asking me that.

"Nothing", I replied arrogantly.

"Shall I ask you for something?"

"Say", my mind was releasing its tension by now.

"I am home alone", want to see you? If you can come on cam?" he asked.

I wonder, why he need to ask. He knew that I never let him down with any of his requests.

"I am in office. I will come. Anything for you.When do you want me to come?"

"ASAP, I am in bed."

"I will let you know once I finish my work here for the evening". I completely ignored his "in bed" statement.

"Thank you", he replied. "I will bathe and dress up for you"

I smiled at his cuteness. "No need, I am not coming to finalize things for marriage".

"Yes, you should not. I have already finalized you, my beauty!"

I was blushing now.

"You are flirt. Do you know that?" I said. Go to have your food now. See you soon. Take care.

"I am waiting for my sunshine." he replied.

It all had started when I heard him for the first time after being friends on social site. The next step now was to see my gadget man for the first time.

I had a head bath. Put on my lip gloss and Kajal. It was my all time favorite makeup. I reached Punjab Agricultural University gate no. 3. I was not much into the sort.

Finally, I settled down in a cyber cafe. He was already there. It was our first live chat.

"Hi! do you have cam there?"

"Hi! How are you? Stay patient. They are installing it. Wait for another five minutes". I directed him.

"I am excited," he said.

"Ha Ha ! hope you don't try to come out of the screen seeing me. Spare me, please." I dialogued in the bollywood style.

"Ha Ha, I will control my feelings, he promised."

"That's good. Cam done", I told him.

"Come on yahoo messenger, bye from here", he said.

"Bye" and I signed off from my gmail.

I had no idea of playing yahoo messenger but had somehow managed. It was for him, so I had to.

"Send me your cam." There is just one displaying my image, he said.

"Hi!, you there?" I asked him.

"Hey, you look beautiful". He was astonished.

"Thanks, where is your cam?" I asked.

"Let me do something with you first. Then I will send you my cam."

"I am going from here then, stop being kiddies." I said.

"All right, I've sent, accept it and then you will be able to view my cam." Was his next message.

"Yes, I did. You should really grow up, Meethu."

"I will, If you take me in your lap."

All sitting in cyber cafe were smiling seeing me laughing at his teaser. But they got busy with their chats later on, having no idea of my laughter.

"Shall I lay or sit?" he asked.

"Do both". I was seeing him tossing in bed.

"You will manage? I do lack this much stamina."

I looked at him. He turned his face and laughed. His eyes half sealed.

I had to say nothing. I laughed like a giant.

"Hey, what is this? Helmet, is it yours?"

"No, I had borrowed it from someone, you need." I asked.

"Ha Ha! I am not coming out there to kiss you, muahhh. You look hot when angry." he typed.

"Who knows? if you will come and smooch."

"You are seducing me, no?"

"You are eager, no..?" I typed with smileys.

We were mad to discuss all this. But he was smiling after many days.

"Please, it's the first time I have got a chance to see you, let me sit and stare at your smile. I love it Meethu". I requested him.

"Oh ! Is it so, Please wear this helmet for me once. Let me see how my Katrina looks Karina in helmet."

"Anything for you". I did but later found all laughing at my dull mind in the cyber cafe. I held the helmet in my hand to ignore this.

"Thanks, you are looking like Katrina Kaif. Beautiful you are to the core."

"Yes, I know. But I love to be myself. I am compared to none. For you, I am happy being your Gudia."

"Thanks for coming. If you can, please stay for some more time," he said.

"No thanks, please. I have to leave, Good night. Take care of yourself," I typed.

After that night, he was in comfort zone. Though I never waited for him, he rang almost every day. I was clown to make him laugh. I loved seeing him smile. He was always alone. I was alone without him. He had worries and success. He had no pleasure in life. He was confined to his dealing with me. To the contrary, I was an open book for him.

His presence was a reason for me to live life. I had no life otherwise. His life had me. He had poured out his heart once. He could cook food. He did all the things himself. He once had an accident. He had no one to take care of him. He had no one to talk to. His lot was pathetic.

I wish, I could fly the distance to be with him. I was human first. I had no mind to be his someone but my concern was to take care of my someone special. When he used to get upset, he always rushed to the temple. He had money but it never bought him any comfort. I had a habit of saving pain of others to my heart. I was rich at heart. I could buy smiles with that. I could let him dump his sadness in the chambers of my heart.

Though nothing related but an experience crossed my mind. I had seen one girl being raped. She lay nude by the roadside. The spectators had interest in mere watching the show. No one had bothered even to cover her up. I was so upset that I went piercing the mob. It had given me courage to lend help to that body. I had spared my salary. I knew she was in need. I could not buy her the lost honor. I could help her to heal wounds though.

I had met another girl once in an auto rickshaw. She was a sex worker. Like all of us, she was doing her job. If I would have been there, playing her role, it would have been hell. Because she had HIV AIDS and could not survive. All the help I offered her was sheer wastage thus.

Meethu J. was someone whom I had regarded the most. People in my life had always advised me to stay in limits with him. I left everyone to be with him. It was less of love and more of devotion.

Sometimes, I used to wonder. He had no one in his life. But he was not taking any initiative. He was passing time with every girl, taking them as friends. I was one amongst them. He had authority to make me attend to his call anytime. Thus one morning, I received his call.

"Good morning", he said.

"Hmmm... good morning. Are you ok? What makes you call at this hour of the day?"

"Thanks, I am good. I was missing you. Love you."

"Love you, too, Meethu J. All are asleep. Can't talk."

"You can listen to me. You won't be able to reply," he said.

I was in his colors.

"I will come and hug you. I will hold you closer to kiss you. I will make you mine. Shall I comfort you in my lap?", he asked.

"Yes", I replied.

"You look more pretty tossing in bed," he said.

I was not able to open the socket of my eyes. It was a real dream.

Now, he was believing in love the way I had always dreamt him to crave for. The huge distance parting us had now been abandoned by the love that truss us.

But all of a sudden, "Hey I will call you this evening. he said. I am going to work." My fantasy was really a fantasy. He was at fault.

I had always entertained his requests. It was the first time he went beyond soul. I wish he would never have regretted, if it was love.

I do things only if I find them right. But I am always right. I never do regret later. Time is the real culprit. I must admit.

Sonio neeni puri kari jande ho

Ehne vadia tuhade shonu monu

Ohna nu ainve dabai jande ho

Sidhe ho ke leto beta

His text message blinked on my screen. He wanted to make me laugh. As he meant, that to sleep at ease, I should not lay with bosom down my body.

Chapter 7

"We formed questions but with no answers."

"Isn't it painful to vomit? It really pains." he said.

"Yes, it really do." I replied.

"It's the most painful thing I have been through", I added.

"You must take care. You are alone there. Who will take care of you", I asked him.

Then we laughed at our chosen topic, to converse. We could pick up the smallest or the biggest things for discussion and debate. It had one thing in common. It was love. I was going more concerned day by day.We had so much to talk. Even the next day's discussion was decided in prior. We use to chat for hours together.

I could send him instant message finding him online.

"Love you."

"I am Ujwal, his friend."

After typing, "I am sorry, I used to log out of my gmail account."

He had always criticised but it helped me learn. Every time I had a new me out of old me. Whatever I have to say, he had one or the other thing against. He was mature enough but seeing him as the wonderful kid next door was what I had out of him with all my pranks and love.

He was hesitant to approve of my love. He had never confessed the same. He never left me. He was not with me even. All he wanted me to do was to be with him. I was aware of his burdened shoulders. I had lessened this with my radiant and comic stories. He had loved his present family. He had ignored planning about his future family. He had spoiled his today to ruin his tomorrow.

He was never wrong.

I was always right.

For a moment, I was silent to feel his words.

After a pause, "yes, you there?" he asked.

"You are too much," I said.

"See, You are blushing," he said.

"Yes, wish you happiness for the day ahead". I replied.

I wish to be a Sadhu", he confessed his loneliness had him, left alone.

"I will be your devotee, right? You and I will preach of sex." I tried making him smile.

"Will you teach me this, too?" he asked.

"We will teach each other", I smiled.

"Is it so, I will love you but in bedroom." he laughed saying this.

"Shut up, you are mad." I went attentive.

"You are wild", he said laughing at me.

"Good day, I have to rush to class now." bye.

"Which class, of sex? Wait for me at least." he cracked again.

As my teacher could not spare me more time, I disconnected the call. "Love you, Call you later", was all I could say.

He had been doing so much for all. Now the time was for all to fetch him felicity because he was deserving more than what they were doing.

The best was predicting his smile, I smiled with him too. I never tried to find anything out of such talks. I never had to hurt him. I never did this to anyone. I knew, how special he was to me.

Chapter 8

"To Love him was Love but
I never loved him as my Love".

His smile was loved. It was love but not *Love*. It captured my attention crusading me to ignore my work. My stupid jokes were the reasons for his smile. I had respect for him. But for self, I had preferred staying his jester.

Whenever, his number use to blink on my phone's screen I had to rush out of my morning MBA coaching class. It was good to skip something for my everything.

"Excuse me Mam", I requested to attend to his call.

"Yes Gudia", she answered politely.

"Good morning, the day had a good start when with you", he said.

Attending to his call was like reverence for him alone.

"Good morning", its my exam today. I told him.

"Good luck," he replied.

"Thanks. Take care and have food, too."

"I will, if you will feed," he said.

"Yes, Look who is there behind?" I use to say this occasionally.

"Please, come and hug me from behind," he said.

"Do you have a boyfriend or a baby to whom you talk to every morning?" my friends inquired.

"Yes, I talk to my baby."

All smirked at this.

Why did he call me every day? I had clustered all smiles, happiness and laughter for his lips. It was the only reason, we were together.

I was crusader, he had known my nerves very well by now.

We discuss now veg of the non-veg stuff. It was like girding one's instinct for going deep into the waters but remaining dry, too. Propitious were the ones who had same tastes. He played pranks and so did I. He joined me for being loyal.

I had not ended a day without him. I loved him but never to admit. I knew his family had not let him dare his ritual and culture. The gadget man defend by his own means.

In his family, people were still in love with *ghisi*, a traditional way of cleaning shit. But they were ultra modern in their means too.

Uttaranchal had been named Uttarakhand. Names were revolutionised but never do the namesake. He was the one who had to bear all this being a pahari boy.

Chapter 9

"Hints here belong to questions but not to answers."

My heart failed to rapport the relation I share with him. I had not been able to tell anyone the same. I had not even wished to explain this. This was like, to gather all hints to find no answer but to get dragged to confusions alone. Our chat was to care each other. We had not dared to commit our commitment for love.

"The best way to predict future is to invent it".

"What were you doing?" he asked.

"How are you? I was missing you, my Meethu."

"I am good. I was seeing your pictures. Love you", he replied.

"Love you, too. You seem low. What happened?" I had a habit of seeing him smile only. I could sense his nerve. His serious tone was driving me mad.

"I always admire if girls are respected. Putting pictures at social site could bring you harm. I love you. I had wished you to be mine. Lock the pictures or else remove."

"I had kept the pictures hidden. Only you will have access. I had shared it else with girls from my friend list." I assured him.

A few days later, a girl had a fake ID by my name. It shared my pictures on public profile. Putting a song of Katrina Kaif. It had my cell number for viewers to contact me on this social website, facebook.

I had no idea about such stupidity until I received a call.

"Hello" it was from an unknown number.

"Yes", I replied, "Who's this?"

"Is this Gudia?"

"You tell your name first", it bothered me too much.

"You had an account on this social site (facebook), as J. Gudia. Kindly check."

I went crazy, finding the same ID existing. It had to be deleted somehow.

I was distorted to tell him anything.

But when discussed, he asked me to complain it as a cyber crime. Unfortunately, our city police had no such assistance to provide. It had to be probed somehow. One of my friends guided me for the same. I had to wait and request my friends to report abuse for the same. It was the only solution I had in hand. As the fake ID gets blocked this way.

He used to call me all the time. He was with me through this hell. I had no idea why he had devoted time to my problem. It all ended in peace. The site did the needful. The fake ID was deleted.

"Only legs don't make one move on in life. Most of the times, it is courage".

I had survived an accident. But it broke my knee joint. More of the trauma was to be suspected of Blood Cancer. The clotting had been the reason behind. Doctor had approved of it, deteriorating my health thus. I had no mind to go for a checkup. I was scared to face this. The thoughts of having it or not, plunged my mind. It was weird but keeping busy all the time was the best option I had left now with me. I was turning coward.

Once he rang to find me crying. I clinched my heart in ribs, accumulated my tongue, to prove things going as usual. I had him passing me his fret. It was odd to pass him mine. I was tensed. Still I had no intention of adding more to his worries, letting him know about this.

At last, he won to know.

"This is not done. Why you never told me?"

"What if it is true?" I sobbed.

"But what if it is not", he asked.

"I don't know", how shall I brave this? I asked him.

"You are strong enough to handle this. I believe you are as normal as I am. Please don't take it to your heart. Keep your head at work to deal with this menace. You will be safe. Please go for the detailed checkup".

"Yes, I will go. Let me arrange few things." I replied.

"When will you go? I am with you always", he said.

"Soon, I will. Thank you so much for your kind support." Earlier, I had been going for leg treatment. Now I had to pull my heart's leg. I had to act sturdy.

"I need you", he said.

Life had another test for me now. The laboratory

was enormous but to make my heart diminutive.

"How much for this test", I pointed to the paper.

"Cancer, which one?", the person on reception desk asked with perfect ease.

"Blood cancer", I mentioned the name of the doctor who had referred.

"You need to wait for your turn", he said. He had to seek permission from his senior doctor for the same.

For then, I ran to escape. In the evening, I went again. I had to keep my words. I had promised Meethu my visit for the test. My bruises had haunted me. I knew, I will sink or float.

My veins and arteries had coagulated the red liquid. I had the report in hand. It was negative. It had normal reasons, can be cured with medicine the doctor had said. I cried out of happiness.

He was happy. He had loved me with his unseen and unknown presence. It was love. It was true to the core.

Once, he had pain due to the stones he had. He was admitted to the hospital. It was tough for him to drive a car.

I told him, "You are stupid. You have what you never expected. You will long to have more. This will never end. Go and get married. You are growing old." I had almost cried.

"Love only those who are meant for love,

Gadgets never say, love you too."

I wanted him having at least the basic of comforts,

a man of his age should be blessed with. He was less bothered about this. I was more concerned somehow.

He once had discussed with me about one of the marriage proposals he had for him.

"Go ahead, if she will not love. You do love her." I told him.

"No one can love me like you do. I can't make one love me. She should do so herself."

"If you will keep on lingering. You will have less of the choices." I went serious discussing it.

"I am confused. I am paying much attention to everything", he replied.

"Yes, You are perfect. But still, you are different. All are not alike. What you are looking for is out of my mind. You send me to coma every time you had a minor to major headache", I said.

"I can't come and nurture you with my love." I told him.

"Tell me if I can find you a heroine", I sniggered.

"You are my heroine", his familiar voice always put me to shivering. His comments make and shake my world, where I had him as my gadget man.

"I have learned to care people too much,

Not because they should care for me.

But because I had known the pain of being ignored"

He had been in love with all my pictures of *karvachauth*.

"This *mehndi* looks good in your hands. Thanks for putting it", he said.

Chapter 10

"You are the one."

"May God's worthiest grace bequeath upon thee",

As he tested thee to be sensible and right.

As opening the lids wide,

Saw a face with all the elegance and pride.

Perceiving a virgin as you are,

A fair and lucid cloud.

It emerged to the mind,

As if he had all to that can't be screamed loud.

As pondering over him, one sensed and alleged,

Thy face is sheen,

Is not phony but is authentic hence so bright,

Thou had seen abruptly a same sight.

As you are the one impersonating one and all's plight,

May you illuminate always as the sparkling night.

Truly contended to see you,

As you are a universal single yet as one's imaginary tough and gallant Knight.

Place your morale elevated,

Firm your decision,

Observing a grip that's stretched as well as tight.

One day you will be the survivor but there will be none to dare you to fight.

May God's worthiest grace bequeath upon thee,

As he tested thee to be sensible and right.

"You are the best. These words belong to you. I wish you all the best for your every future endeavour. You will be the one to conquer this world. You will have everything at your disposal. Trust me, I prayed for your success. God had ensured me this. You will always be the reason for me to try and make you smile.'

After ages, I had pen down something. I would never have cracked this without him. I loved my words, reason – they speak of him. My writing had him. He was in my writings.

"For him, this pen runs...

Grace of God is never left under shade,
It had hues too and darkness that surely fades.
But the real trust is if you are left in lurch,
Stay there with all the satisfaction as if in church.
He loves you that's right and may never let you cry,
If he had started life as blank, but will paint the end bright.
You need to know that a while had passed cursing Him,
He was busy with nothing but to end your tears with a sweet smile.'

I had never dedicated my words to anyone. I had him. He, who drove me to write more and more. I was happy with him. He had the best out of me.

It marked the beginning of something, I had not wished it to end now, but for him alone.

Chapter 11

"Pranks are for kids, even for those who stay silent in a matured heart".

He could not help but laugh when I had promised organising cycle rally in his honour. He had to visit India. It would have been his visit after two years. I had no mind of seeing him. I knew he was alone, it will lead him to take my care and love otherwise. He may mess up everything. I wanted to be his, for lifelong. The way I was, I was happy to be. Man crafts bewilderment.

"Did I tell you something about cycle episode?" he asked.

"No, but I am waiting to hear." I asked as if I was really interested to know.

"Once I had kept a bicycle lock around one guy's neck and had thrown the keys. He couldn't unlock it. He was helpless. We had a day of fun and frolic. My teacher had asked me to bring parents along the next day in school.

You know, my dad did more of the crap. He told the teacher, it's their age to do such things. We, the aged and old are not made for pranks." He laughed heartidly telling me this.

It was his first Subway store. He had done so much to own this. He had his training. I knew I will miss him during this stay. He was to stay at his friend's place. I received his unexpected call one night.

"Hi, I had a rough throat. Sorry, I got so busy. I should have called", he said.

"No, it's all right. But you should have at least messaged. Someone was dying for you here", I replied.

"Hey, don't say that. Who is dying?" he asked in a mock tone.

"I don't know." I got angry. "I will disconnect the call and you will know, about whom I am talking I said."

"Sorry, please." he said.

"I never ask you to divert your mind from your work. But at least bother about the one who is..." I directed him to *guzzle* honey, garlic and *mulatthi*. "It would soothe your throat", I said.

Later, he managed calling me. When all used to get busy with their chores, stealthily he would dial my number and with our little anecdotes we used to laugh all night.

We used to say, 'love you', a million times a day. But it was more of the dedication. Every time, it had a meaning.

He had managed his subway the best way. He used to call everyone, family, friends and of course me. He was good at managing time. I never needed his time, but the moments when he really was with me. He was not good at telling lies. He had shared his casual pictures by now.

It was nothing more of a prank, when he had sent me a picture. It engrossed us together. We were in blue outfits.

"See, what I did last night?" he said laughing.

"It is beautiful feeling to receive such gift from your dream boy. I will make it more beautiful for you," I said.

I forwarded him many of the pictures. Those were different in forms. But one thing that was similar in all the pictures, was us.

Chapter 12

"Begin an unending began"

"I am coming to India. Will you come to receive me at station? Will you come, jump and hug me?"

I was about to say, "I will come and kiss you, too. Collecting myself, I said, "No, I won't see you". I am sorry."

"What are you saying? I am coming on this Diwali", he said.

"Yes, I will be happy if you come. But I will not be glad seeing you." All will not be, I thought. I had known the art of consoling but not hurting. I knew it was best to say no now, than to get no later on from him.

"I know you are kidding", he said. He was sure of meeting me. He knew I had never said no to him for anything.

"Ok, I will see you. You are really a kid." I said.

I had loved this festival of lights, since childhood. I had seen God remaining unbiased on this day. HE lit every nook and corner. Every heart had a spark. I could devote hours to enjoy this luxury of happiness. I felt as if I had stars on earth. I wonder if I could find one I had lost.

After the accident, it was recovery time for me now.

I had been going for physiotherapy. I never knew God had him as my doctor. His visit was going to ensure my speedy recovery. I would not have known it. I had waited for him.

I was waiting for someone I knew very well who knows me, too. But we were not knowing what we were to each other.

Chapter 13

"To see or not to."

I knew he had landed on this earth of emotions by now. He was in India. His phone was switched off. I had not headache but *mindache*. On my way to home, I sent him a message, "Hope you are safe." I was going back from my morning MBA class.

"How is your *tangri* (leg)?" It made me smile. But the next line of the message vanished it." *Tagdi* roaming, catch you soon." He wrote just these two lines in the message.

I wonder, why do I hurt my poor heart for the one, who doesn't know it beats for him alone.

I had no other message and call. I could not sleep in peace. I rang his father expecting Meethu to attend to the call. It was my care, I had done this way for him always.

It was another morning, I had a call from a landline phone number. I was in office. Hoping it to be of a client's number, I picked up.

"Hello, Good morning." I was polite, expecting it to be a customer call of spa and salon, I was working in.

"Hi, How are you?" He was cheerful.

"Hey, How are you? Did you reach safely? I am better than you. I should not speak to you. I couldn't sleep last night." I said everything in one stretch.

"But I didn't come to disturb you in bed. I was tired. Else you know me, no..? I want to see you tonight, if you say."

I smiled but curbed it. "Why shall I continue speaking to you? I will not see you. I had told you this prior, too." I replied.

"It's been almost two days, now see what are you saying? Please", he went meek.

"You are very bad", I said

"But good in bed", he smiled.

I had always loved seeing him smile. I could not defend him more. "I will see you soon". I was going to die, I knew without him.

"Come in salwar suit." I had received his message.

"I will come but why so much of the formalities."

"I like to see you that way", he said.

"Oh ! I will do that." I said.

"Hey ! I wish I had asked you to come in bikini. You never say me no. no..?"

"Yes."

"Means, if I say, you will come?"

"No."

"Say, yes or no."

"Whatever."

"You come as you want, I will do the rest", he said.

I smiled.

* * *

It was Diwali. I had seen kids playing in streets cracking crackers. It was the best festival, I was in love with. I had to reach office. Staff had to arrange for *Diwali Poojan*. We had to lit *diyas*. We had to offer prayers too.

"See you today", "Come in salwar suit", came his text message on phone.

I did not reply. Moreover, it made me angry. He had been sending same messages since he came. I had to ignore this today, too. I had to smile this day. I had to make others smile. I managed to be at office. I had taken my brother along. I was not able to drive my scooter because of nothing but the knee-joint's pain.

He rang me to inquire the address. I went near the window pane.

"Is the building near Nokia store", he asked.

"Yes, this is the building." I shouted aloud. It was a big surprise. He was parking his bike. I went near the stairs to receive him.

I could see my gadgetman out of the gadget box finally. It was November 05, 2010.

I hugged him as tight as I could. He wrapped me in his arms. I wished this moment to be everlasting. I kept staring at him. It was my dream that has come true, meeting him.

Once more, he had spread his arms. But I shrugged my shoulders.

He, too, had been conscious of the beings around by now.

"This is for you, Gudia". He passed me a pack of chocolates.

"Thanks, I don't need this. You are the precious gift." I had no gifts for him. I had already distributed the things to kids that I had for him. Reason, he kept lingering visiting. He had not even asked me to come and see him. I knew the reason.

I seated by his side. I was going to crumple any moment. I had not gathered such happiness ever. I had to hold his hands to realise it was in real. I have seen him in dreams. It was a real dream. I had God's best gift received.

After the shy eyes encounter halted, I asked him for water.

"Yes, I will have only if filtered", he said.

I had to manage standing straight. My knee joint still twisted to pain. I hobbled.

He slapped me as I stood to fetch him water. *Ptak*, (a sound of pating) he *sniggered*.

I laughed on my way to pantry. I remember, we have decided to be informal. We have to be as we were always, less than lovers but more than friends.

'Water, It's pure.' I smiled.

"Excellent!", he said.

I did prayers as per our rituals and had given him *prashad*.

He was to leave. I swallowed the lump down my throat. To bid him bye for now was a must. I wanted to be with him. I had no wish to say anything to him.

I went closer to pull his cheeks. He firmly slapped my hands on my face. He received call from home. He had to be back by now.

"All right. Do inform of your well-being as you reach." I told him.

I embraced him again. In my heart, I chanted prayers. God bless him, Please. My God was in my prayers. He never knew what he had given me. I had not expected anything more.

But he was ready to medal my love.

Still, I was to go home. My phone beeped. It was his message.

"I shy, you cute, so many people

You look good, I cute, love you beta."

I was smiling in silence. I came home and relished the sweetness of his love in chocolates he had for me.

I had to peep inside my mind. Heart had him inside its chambers. The story had its origin around the orthodox beings. I was optimist but not the one of their kind. Still I had my rules, not to hurt. Even the ones who hurt you are befuddled at your smile. His family can never come forth to accept a girl, if not a Kumauni.

Chapter 14

"I was someone else when I was with him,

Someone more like myself."

The very next day I had him again in my office. I could find him sitting inside my cabin. I came out of washroom to welcome him. Still an hour was more for the day, left at work. I was surprised to see him that evening.

"Hi, nice dress *beta*", he said.

"Thanks. How come you here, without any message?" I replied.

"Sorry, Did I disturb your work?" he asked.

"No, not at all." I wanted to keep my finger on his lips. He had disturbed me with his presence though. I wanted to ignore this interaction. I had no mind of hurting him with my words.

"Water or tea?" I asked.

"You", he said. "I will drop you home. Let us go for a ride."

"Now?", I went pale but asked him.

"Yes, any problem?" he asked.

"Not with me." But with my poor heart. I didn't say though. "Ok. Let us have a cup of tea for the time being." I offered an option.

"We should leave. You have to be home on time. Give me your bag", he said.

"We came down in lift. He ensured, I sat in comfort.

* * *

The ride on road somehow had been thrilled by his presence alone.

We kept laughing. He crossed the road leading to my place. I sat at a distance in his car.

"You should take a turn from here", I said.

"You are forgetting something", he said.

"What?" I was not aware of his intentions.

He was a lover of the present, he had always ignored his past. But now he was reminding me of something. He had to cite here one of the chats. I had promised to hug and kiss him. I had done the former, he was indirectly asking me for latter.

"How is everyone home?" I still ignored his request.

"Say? you always keep your word", he repeated.

I was perplexed. I had never been with any guy in a car ever. For him, what more I had to do now? I somehow made up my mind to kiss, hesitated a thousand times. Before I proceed, I had to have courage.

I leaned on his shoulder. I hugged. This was the comfort of heaven. It was likely driving me his devotee.

He didn't know that I was pondering my love for him or if he had felt the same, too.

As I was going to touch his cheeks with my lips, he turned though, unknowingly to say something. His lips joined mine. I closed eyes to this and opened customs to be his. It was the origin. We kept roaming on roads by then.

We had come closer more than friends less than lovers. It was fusion of confusion.

His lips, still rested on my lips. He had his hands evading my chastity, overpowering my soul. I hadn't resisted neither had I surrendered, swayed by his every touch to melt in his arms.

It had thrilled each of my nerves. I gave up myself to be his someone.

He had taught me one lesson, I had never been aware of.

"Sex was important."

While dogs chased the car, We were chasing each other.

Chapter 15

"Given same flesh would have solved it,

Let it be otherwise,

God created social animal, but animal."

"We need to experience bike, too. All the days are not alike, I wish you are not addicted to car alone. Please hold me firmly", he said. He had come on his old motorbike. We had plans to pay visit to temple as well as Gurudwara.

I never had any reply to such things. I was afraid of something.

We were to temple. He clasped my hands to help me go upstairs. It was a huge ambiance. It took an hour for us to pray. It was named after Shri Krishanji, a mythological God.

He handled the polybag on his bike. It was serenity. I had loved him more. He was behaving somewhat like me now. He was unique in his ways.

We went to Gurudwara Sahib, too. It was the day to visit God with my God. He was penetrating inside me and my heart. He was going deep inside my eyes. He didn't let me join my colleagues to go downstairs. He went to washroom to delay our moving out of office, when we were back from Gurudwara Sahib.

I felt strange in love with him. I hadn't hesitated. I had joined his passion. He had me in his wrap and kissed me passionately.It was the second time in my life since I met him. I had no wish to count this love for.

"What you asked God for?" he said this to make me feel comfortable after this long love making moment.

"I ask God to bless all with happiness." I replied

"Have not you asked something for yourself?", he inquired.

"I am in all. If all are happy, so am I."

I could not let a single event of his glimpse go waste.

"Go home and message me." I directed him.

I had his message. 'I wished God to give me you, if you are mine. If not, I had requested them to make it so.' he said.

I could not tell him anything. I had seen him crying alone. I had wishes for him to get settled in life.

'I had seen him through ups and downs,

I had seen him through thick and thin,

I had seen him this and that,

I can see him with his eyes alone.'

"I reached safely. Good night." I replied.

I was left alone with him somewhere in my oblivion mind.

* * *

He was with me almost every day. I had to love him. I was hurt of being in an unknown relation. It was unsaid, unseen and unknown but unpredictable love too.

"Am I a driver? Shall I keep driving this way?

He grumbled as we went for a drive.

"What do I say? Let me drive", I said.

"You come and sit in my lap to do so", he dazzled.

He was angry now.

He wanted to love and be loved. But a driver, unattended, was not his choice.

I smiled and it irritated him more.

I had been a social animal for his sake. I loved him. I had to do so. I had to be in his colors.

"See", I pointed to a dog watching us from outside the car to change his mood.

"Yes, he is to learn watching us, his style."

"What is this new thing now?" I laughed.

"You don't know?", he questioned.

"Nope", I was smiling but knowing his intentions somehow.

"I will tell you, live. It's like", he smiled and burst to laughter, without saying anything more than this.

I, too, laughed. His smile was beautiful than my stupid mind jolting to find the exact sense out of this talk.

Chapter 16

"Leaving all the pains behind..."

I was bathed. He was standing outside my place. We had to go for one of the trips. He was on time. I was late as usual.

After few minutes, we were riding our hearts on highway. He had asked me a day before to join him for this. I had agreed. He was alone. I was alone without him. I had almost ignored my work for accompanying him. He was no one but someone, I could not now live without.

He used to ask, 'yes or no.'

Yes, was always my reply. He was used to of this 'yes' now.

It took me hours to convince my parents to join a strange friend from strange lands for a strange journey. All were strangers, but he was not.

We had our morning tea at roadside *dhaba*.

"See, that man is staring", I complained.

"You are also looking at him", he answered.

"Hey, he is smiling." I shouted.

"You don't then", it was a simple end reply, he had.

He was cute to scold me for throwing out the empty bottles on road. I was sorry for my little mistakes.

All mornings do bring dawn, it was not one of the kinds but. Everything was beautiful, best, charming, because of his presence. The roads, meádows, morning time had gone exotic. I was with him. He turned beautiful than everything else in this world by now.

Even the naturalistic beauty need not be admired, when the arresting one has captured you with all the seductiveness of mellow wines. I was not petrified of him, anymore. I had not been with any guy in such a way. He was above everyone. He was more than my self-respect too. I had my rules at stake. I had new rules. I was his follower to follow the newly set ones, rules.

We flew towards our destined halt. I lay on his shoulder to feel blessed again, borne out of my ashes. He placed my hands around him and had hugged me and kissed me on forehead. I did the same. I knew my limits, I respect him. If he didn't like my loving him, if he takes me wrong, I was doing this right thing wrongly. I had this furnace burning within. I had not loved him. I had him as my love.

Few memories flashed in mind.

He had been in love with family. He was caring for surrounded beings. He was helping his life, too. He had been thinking of all, he was to be thought of for now. He had to see girls for match. He was here for marriage. I was the only girl he had been with. He had been through this all. He had to ditch a girl for the sake of rituals. I knew how he had faced life. When that girl had invited him for her marriage, he couldn't face it. But he was the one, who let her face this for life.

I had to give him a gift, worth his life demanded for. I had love and care. It was his riches, I had.

* * *

His shy smile resembled much to his presence in my dreams. He had pain. It was due to stones he had. I had all the things to say to divert his mind from the pain, he was suffering alone.

I prayed to Goddess to pass all his pains to me. He should be happier than anyone else around.

"I want to see all the mountains. You wait and watch", he said.

We did *jai jai* at *Chintpurni mata*, I clicked few of his photographs. He, too, clicked few while I distributed *prashad*.

We stayed and prayed there together. "I had my God with me now, thanks, in my heart", I said.

What he would have asked, God here. He had messaged me when he had been to *Krishna mandir*.

"I want to carry your handbag this way forever", he had hugged me so tight that I had to hug him the same way. I had ignored it many times though.

"We can't take *prashad* along from here. It is a hearsay". I paid more attention to what he was telling. I knew it but I loved being a learner again for him.

He had much of the pain because of his stone problem and I had due to much walking and stressed knee joint. "All will take us wrong, check how do we walk?" he said.

I smiled, I never had to handle such tough things.

It was to caress his smiles and to fake my smile, too. We went to a shop, where he helped me go upstairs to washroom, and removing our shoes, we went together to wash hands.

It was like in heaven, with him.

Jai Mata Di, all were bowing heads in regard. We, too, joined them, reaching the place of superpowers. 'May all forget to cry, wish they are in love with smiles.'

It was crowd waiting for the gates to open for prayer. We sat in one corner, he lay in my lap. I consoled his pain caressing his hair and massaging his head. His pouted upper lip made him a kid, I was in love with.

Seeing him in pain was the worst pain for me. Every time he raised his brow, I cursed myself for this forced trip.

My leg was not able to let his head rest on its strength. I had to help him saying, *Jai mata di*, it had helped me so much too. It may have deprived him of his pain too.

Do God give someone this wonderful reason ever in life to love the one you love in public without any hesitation, without heeding attention to the gathered mob around, but to peep deep into the love swayed by its beautiful feeling. I wish it to happen everyday. I had love for him and that love lay smoldering within, he was not tossing, but lay still, wearing the less black, more of grayish T-shirt. I had noticed that even he needed this love, he had seen people but they didn't belong to him in Australia where he was staying.

"Crowd doesn't ensure you are occupied with their presence, a mob is never a company".

He woke up after half an hour.

"How is your pain?" I asked

"Less than before, but it's still there", he replied. No one had loved the way I was loving him, no one had taught me but mere absence of love did, to love the one's I loved, he was the first and last in list.

He woke up. A lady inquired, whom we told that he had pain.

Being Indian but hospitable, she told us to get medicine when in market and that, too, will help. It reminded me of our halt mid way to buy medicine. Even at *Chintpurni mata*, I scolded myself for this stupidity of asking him to continue trip with this pain.

We did *jai jai*. I had asked God to pass his pains to me. I was more good at handling this. He didn't know, his love had sweet pain for me.

We came out and clicked more pictures to keep memories. We were going back to Ludhiana. With his single handed driving skills, we were blessed to be here together, praying for causes.

We had seen the beauty of nature, it was always tempting, but he pampered more than those sights. He had to seek a point to sit and let me stare at him. I had closed my eyes now, he had his arms around, and had dragged me as close as possible, we were two souls mingled one as through the blood in flee.

We had now reached plains leaving behind the mountains that lured us. He wanted to go back again as we had not sat on *phars*, he wished to sit by my side there.

We reached at one place where few of the cows grazed. We had parked car to soothe our eyes with the scenic beauty, my eyes had him as the one I was in love with.

It was *rancho baba*. He had pierced my heart but I had curbed my passion to be with him with solemn respect I had, because I had seen him going through tough situations where he lacked the attention to hold it firm.

He came to hold me but I denied with a slight push. It had happened thrice, finally I surrendered, I had love for him but was petrified, where to run and how?

Later I smiled seeing him turned red, transient his hues turning me to crimson, too. If this is love, I do wonder, but yes, it had made me feel that I had never felt even when watching such things happening in Hollywood and Bollywood movies.

We reached Ludhiana, chatting and making love the one way or the other, then waited somehow, when ek aari happened many times, finally surrendering my chastity in his honour. He was getting me out of me, I never knew, I was made for this. He taught me that day.

It was important to be denied for what you deny.

There was no one else, whom, I had given such opportunity to teach me all this. The plea to *ekk aari* terrified me the most, his passion to make me feel the natural play in love with dedication. I ended up the way it should have happened.

Finally, the setting sun compelled us to rush home. I asked him if he had a safe drive back to rush home. He had bathed, had food and was going to sleep after his medicine. He messaged that he had left all the pains behind. I had joined him on his way to doctor next day. His turn was still awaited.

I had already drank too much water but before entering, I had to pee, he said.

I laughed, he was kid when with me. Otherwise, he was more of Mr. President. And finally, doctor relieved him of his pain.

Every evening, we had decided to pay visit to *neelkanth* temple, where we had loved prayers. I had my God with me there. I had decided to go there for seven days if we were going otherwise, too. He agreed. It was in oblivion, when with each other we offered prayers, he lent me his hand for helping me go along and reach upstairs with ease. I loved him for doing this for me but in turn I had much to gloze him in and around with my love for him. I received one evening his message, *sorry for I can't come*. It was decided prior that we would pay visits and accordingly he had to go back, too. But his dad was in hospital. He had cardiac arrest, I had to go. I went there to the temple with one of my lady manager and her family, offered prayers, *My dad is not keeping well. This time I had you to help me, God, save him now or I will keep poisoning my life for not too able this time too.* I came back home and asked him about dad's well being.

He said, "They need an operation". He had asked doctor, 'what would be best, do that, please?'

I couldn't let him stay this way, I went to see him when he was little free after all the tiring pressure. He had extended his visit. I had more of respect for him for this decision. His work and his business was more hassled. His absence was the reason. He had his mind full of so many things. I met him in hospital parking. He told me that he had cried today.

You need not to because everything is fine by now, I said. I had carried few things. I had no idea but I had always carried gifts of smile alone to give. Was it making me the reason for mockery?

I went and found him sitting quiet and his quiver speech spoke everything to me. I went to see dad, who he was to me otherwise? I wanted my God to bless his father. I had seen his mom by now.

I wanted all to take care of his dad. They did and after few days, he was feeling good and was discharged from hospital to stay home, receiving the love of all.

God in my dream hinted me, his not coming along for *neelkanth* visits was a reason for his stay back. He does his duties the best way.

I respect you, don't know why? Seeing him I had said.

When the next day again I went to see his dad, but had not been able to, he never said to come again. I had no belongingness to show, if he had not wanted me to show. I didn't want to hurt him. I was better aware of this by being hurt, but not do I did this.

Our another trip......

We went to Kasuali. We were talking of things making us more sensible, we had to ignored our pranks for the time being.

To a friend who was staying, back in Chandigarh, I asked, “Angrej, if you are in need of my ipod, he simply denied. “No, you are in need of this.” He had seen Meethu playing *bhajans*.

Hor fer (what else), he had been asking this. “I am sleepy”, I replied.

“Go and sleep at the back seat. If I could wake you up from your sleep, you will join me here again.”

“What if not?” I asked.

“Then I will join you, simple.” he laughed.

It was of laughing material type talks.

I was happy seeing mountains, he, too, was.

I wish if I could take few back to home.

“I will take you along to Uttarakhand, to my village.” he said.

“What will I do there?” I asked.

“It is your village, you love me, that’s all is your job about.” he said.

“That I always want to, but how, and you never say so in a way I could understand at least”. I thought.

Now the beauty of the deep valleys had been diversified as seen from above. But I had not left even a single chance to stare at my world. He caught me so many times doing this, but I could just pass my hand to clear his face. I closed my eyes to switch over to same topic again, ‘sleepy I am.’ I said it almost every time he caught me staring at him.

Both of us were very well aware of what was happening, even what we were doing at this point. It is not wrong, I can't regret, but at the same time, he is supposed to receive my love and care like anyone else this way. We avoided such topics and if he was happy, nothing else I wanted. I had longed to see him smiling with his chinky eyes closed and nothing was compared to this in the world.

When beloved loved lover, the most important, beautiful thing is nothing but to see God in him.

We reached and crossed the sunset point to reach the gates of airforce station to proffer our prayers at Manki Point, a place we had never been to. The way he carried me in arms, I could feel his every touch the same for ages to come. It had given me shivering sensation that was running down my body to feel more of his woman. I was unable to walk the steep hilly upstairs, he took me holding in his arms, close to his heart. With every slight push he brought me close to his soul. It was not tiring but a refreshing experience. Every pain had vanished, *balaji* had his habitat there and we adjured there, bowing our heads down and folding our hands.

Oh balaji, oh shree sankatmochan hanumanji, please help me hold my courage with firm faith and never to give up spirit, and face this cruel ways of world boldly.

He shrugged his shoulders when I told him not to help me go down.

"Why? I will and always will do the same." he said.

"You have already helped me climb but now you must be tired." I said.

"No I am not, are you?" he told and asked in unison.

There were school kids who asked us for lift but we didn't help. I know, to so many even if we wanted, couldn't.

His single hand driving was keeping my love for him alive and it was being received by his another hand too by me.

I had brought something, I wanted him to check if he liked his gift. He had liked it. He stopped the car on the road side and hugged me.

He said, "Remove your coat, Don't you feel it's hot"?

I smiled at him.

He hadn't even cared for the man who had stayed to smoke there, watching us.

He rooted me in arms and I began to get vibes out of him, more than before, kissing me, he closed my eyes and went enhancing my screams as he did love me more and more.

Somehow the man smoking behind started his car altering us of our love making. We too moved out and found a haunted yet artistic place. He went there, it was more of fear and less of excitement but with him I drove my oars to feel happiness in his smiles.

He had his cam, he picturised everything there and interviewed me, too.

The beauty of such mystic place was a million times enhanced when I had seen him getting emerged with this merriment.

I stood there to watch him, "Did he smile this way, in the past ?" I asked myself.

Things crossed my mind, why he had liked me when my knee joint broke and I was facing it all very bravely. He too had felt once the same, meeting with an accident, torturing him to be loved, but to ask whom for it?

He had told me how he had managed to bathe, pray and do justice to his life out of being his sole companion in loneliness.

He had not celebrated his birthday, with whom he would have done so ?

He had no one to share his happiness with, receiving birthday presents if ever given.

I had known him from the times he was struggling, when he had nowhere to stay at in peace, when he had nothing known as the happiness. I had congratulated him for his approval for the subway and he opened it after he had undergone training for the same. He deserved this time to be full played. He deserved, everything a man of his age did. He deserved to be loved by his wife.

I opened my eyes to wake up from this thought. He went near the running water and I joined him. We sat and were happy at the discovery of this wonderland. It was comfy being with him when the pool around had spread its chilled waves in the breeze.

He had no mind of moving out of this place, he had never dreamt of, but we had to, before sunset. We left to carry memories and even to leave few of them for the comimg times to cherish. I had never seen him this much resilient. His fragrance had wrapped me, casting a spell.

Again, we have reached our town to let the dogs see why we are not posing as they do, he said as we entered the city.

I smiled.

He had given me so much out of his stay, that now I had no mind of thinking if his faith on me would ever shake.

We had touched and trapped each of the barren roads and meadows. We had been to Govind Goo Dham too. I was into such prayers that he would have not even thought of. I had loved the love of *Radha Rani for Shri Krishanji*.

Now, I Had been in love with my *laddoo gopal ji*.

I had been to *Sai Dham*, where *sabka malik ek* was chanted, he was the one for me too now.

Now came the time for him to leave for Australia, leaving with me his incredible presence. 'I will miss you', saying this I had cried. He made me laugh saying, 'I will come again for a heart beat check up'.

It reminded me of the day, he had sat in my office waiting for me to get free with my work. He had brought me the *parshad* from *prabhat pheri*.

"Sit, please." I said.

"Give me some time", I had to deliver products to my staff, they are attending customers, I said.

"Oh! Is it so", he asked.

I replied, Yes, it is.

You are cute Gudia", he said.

As I sat there to trim cotton, he came close and my eyes had nothing to see but to feel him kissing, his hands exposing my femininity.

"Hey, it's my fast today." I said.

He said, "God had exceptions in love." He continued his passion, seducing me more than ever.

He wanted me to provide him with my *kundli*. He went for a photostat, but came back again. With the sccissor, I had cut my finger, he had bandage with him for me that he had bought.

"Let me first check your heart beat", he extended his hands across the table to reach me. He was sitting at another corner of the table. I stood and ran, and he chased me to give me bandage. I took one and thanked and ran again. Like a childplay, it was good seeing him everytime with smiles, that he had lost somewhere earlier.

As I comforted my finger with bandage and bent to pick up the packaging, he came from behind and hugged me. His hands were on my bust, his masculinity I felt for the first time. He kissed my neck to see my reaction. I could not move an inch.

This ended hearing tapping of feet at the door of my office. "I will take this photostat then", he said.

All right, see you soon then. I had to lump down this from my throat somehow, bidding him good bye that day.

"Bye" he left.

* * *

As his trip to India now had come to an end. He was leaving, I was crying at heart. I had been seeing him with all my love for him. I smiled sobbing and cleaning my nose.

"You didn't come for firing even, you are my special guest. Do come now", I said.

"I would have come with dad for firing", he replied.

"No issues, you and dad can come", I said.

I had a cake for him, though earlier, he had not received it.

"Adieu, but you are always welcome", I wrote on the cake.

"Third cake, I will smash it on his face, if he deny coming this time", I thought.

I remember how I had planned a surprise lunch for him and he had denied that. He never knew I had this surprise, may be he would have considered otherwise.

"*Akshu*, do you want cake? I will bring chocolate one for you."

He can now take it home, he had cleared his way by asking one of the kids at home, though he had not let the kid reply.

We went for a little ride. He didn't let me pull his cheeks and even hug him. But we did it behind the log of a giant tree, while sitting in the car.

Seeing a man, we rushed. I hugged him many times before finally I had to bid him goodbye.

I had loved him like a mad. A night before his departure, I had felt it tough to hold on, that in actual it was his love. He went crazy, receiving my love. This was the time when I had him in mind and occupying every space in my body and soul.

"Bye ! I am running late" I messaged him. I waited for the day long as he was planning to make me see dad but it didn't happen.

I rang him and his dad attended the call.

"Namaste, come home someday, Sakshi." His father said.

"I will surely drop in someday", Thanks. I said.

"How are you keeping your health, everything is fine, no?" I asked him.

Later I reached home with *angrej* to cry and miss Meethu, messaging him. Angrej was a common friend who had witnessed our love and trips.

When he had to catch his flight. He said, "I will miss you there *beta,* so much.

I too will really miss you". I messaged.

He had not taken anything from me, but he had not left me with anything even. "Thanks for your love", I said.

"Will you love me the same." he asked..

"No, I will not. I said.

............................?

"I will keep on doubling this love." I replied.

"Thanks, *beta.*" he said.

"Take care of yourself and safe journey my love. Always carry this smile. Wish you don't spend a single day without wearing it on your lips." I said.

"Yes, I will." he assured.

"Promise..?" I confirmed.

"Yes, promise, you sleep now." he replied.

Angrej was messaging me to smile. Lots of love. Loads of care. Take care of yourself." I slept messaging him.

He reached safely, I thanked God for this.

Then happened the most important thing in his life. He had everything under control in his Subway and he was happy with this.

He was always here in my heart though the distances lay between us. He had discussed with me about a number of girls, being chosen to be his partner.

It's been years now, are you prolonging it or you want a princess, my prince charming.' I cracked a joke asking him.

We used to share things but the best that I always did was just crying and pouring my heart to him alone. When he told me once about the thing that he loved me too, but he was afraid of the things he had seen at his place. "How it would be possible this way *beta*, he asked?"

"What you had for dinner?" I switched on another topic, had no intentions to see him hurt.

"So much, you tell". he asked.

"Good." I said.

"Love you and take care of yourself."

* * *

Another day and another him. We were chating.

“Will you love me the same always?” he asked

“No”, I had replied.

“Why so?” he was shocked.

“Because I will add more and more love for you.” I replied.

“Will you cook food with your hands?” he threw another question.

“I will, but not of hands. You have to promise that you will not get angry. Receive this love with open arms. I have nothing more to do *beta*.” I told him.

“Promise you will not leave me alone ever.” he asked.

“I will not.” I was lost while replying to him.

I knew he was asking me all this as one of his friends had ended his relationship in an unhappy marriage.

“Never ever *bache*, I understand that your friend had such a bad experience but all this had a reason. All the marriages are different.” I said, assuring I will not leave him alone.

“Few end up this way, others happen to be the memorable ones setting example for others to follow.

“If ever I will get angry, promise me you will not get angry, too.” he asked.

“I will, but will never let you know. I will always love you the way I am madly in love with you.” I said.

“Please hug me, this house is haunting me.” he said.

I was always there for him, I was always his girl.

"Thanks, I had a busy day." he said.

"Oh, is it so? Take rest then." I said.

"Put me to sleep, my baby." he requested.

"I did that but had consoled my poor heart somehow".

"Can you please forward me this song, *surili.*" he requested.

"Yes, a minute, its being uploaded."

"Thanks." he replied.

This was the song, he had always loved singing. He was a good singer. I had heard him singing, *janeman*, pitch next to this word was noted high. He sang so well, I had my Indian-cum-Australian idol. 'Will you please sing this song', I used to say. He was less caring about lyrics, *Surili akhiyon wale dil kahin khoya hai miyan.*

Kaise mujhe tum . . .

This was done because of the spelling check feature in his phone. For me, every song passed on had a meaning, I thanked God as *tujhe bhula diya* was now replaced with 'I Love You.' Both bolywood songs though.

I had forwarded him the pictures on *picasa album,* of both of us.

It reminded me the day, he was in my office.

'Come on, tell me how this works. He was asking about *Jacuzzi.*'

He had kissed me on cheek when nobody was standing there.

He asked, "How do I open this file? Yes," I had now been able to open. "Thanks, it will remind me of the best time I had just with you during my stay here in India. He could not leave a chance to kiss me and had done it even when everyone was around but busy.

He said, "Promise me, if something happens you will move on."

"I can't say anything now *beta*, love you." I replied.

The real bolt out of the blue was *Haldiwali* or *Haldiwani*.

Everything was going to fix up soon. I had always discussed with him.

I always had wished him to be happy this way or the other. But this time another girl had crushed my brains. I had no idea of seeing my love with unknown girl. 'All are involved in it'. He had told me this. "I can't raise a voice", he said, "Hope you understand."

If maths, would have been easy than I would have created success stories by now, but I had no interest in that.

There were times earlier when I had given up. I had not tried to contact him. He didn't let me continue this. He kept contacting all the time. Finally, I had to be with him.

This time was asking me to pay a price that I was not able to pay for. I had cried on the roads, I had shouted to self. I had alcohol for the first time in my life, even if it was tough to do so. I had later vomited my feelings in front of God. The single sip of alcohol screwed my consciousness. It had burned the material under my *rib cage*.

I thought, "Why can't he take stand to tell, we were in love? Will he be happy with her? I had no idea of going where and doing what.

I went to the temple and had not attended to his call.

The gadgets are invented by people who had thought beyond their perception. The orthodox people should not be given any of the rights to use such gadgets. The self-fight ended. I had decided to ask my father to help me out. The pandit had come to paint my forehead in red. Go home, take rest. God will do the next.

Forever, I will keep on staying with his love, I decided.

I read his message. I don't want to cheat her. I want to be with her.

Then, I replied, "Hope you never need to break her trust." She may trust you as I feel sorry for all that happened, last night. God will bless you with all the happiness in your life *beta*.

I had managed a tough and hard life to fuck my heart. I had to be at temple, staring at God, praying for him. Hope, he is doing all right. I had no courage to face my God. He was my God.

I had quit every interest in life. I had taken interest in life because of him. Without him, it was not a life. I had never dressed the same. I had not been the same. I was what, I was for him alone.

I had left everyone behind, to be with him. Now I was alone but he should not feel it even, it really pains, it really does, I thought one day.

He left me with all the stupid things, I would cry in my class and run from class even when madam was standing in front to teach. I used to go near river, miss him and stay there for hours. I had his presence everywhere, it made me cry all the time, I had urge to commit suicide, jumping into the deep waters. He will be held responsible, I can't do that I thought.

'Gudia smile, it will let God to bless him I could say to self.'

I had my date sheet in hand. I had not attended classes with attentive mind. I had no mind to study but to think of him.

One night, I had messaged him, 'shall we try at least for the last time and if we are made for each other.' God knows. It was again the same social site. I was messaging him from.

I had no idea of receiving his call and reply.

I went to temple and poured out my heart, 'Spend your life alone. No big deal but don't let yourself be a slut. You have the guts to do anything.'

It was the time, I had paid attention to my studies with focus that was more than required. I used to stay busy.

All the time, headphones shove in and I used to fall sleep this way. My health had deteriorated receiving this blow. I received his call on the very first day of my exams but I didn't answer.

'Good luck, thanks. We will try again, I will make my dad understand', his message came.

It baffled me what makes him say so now, I don't know, I could say nothing. I have my exams. I wanted to hug him and cry though.

"You pay full attention to your studies, I will wait, thanks," his next message helped me not to reply.

He used to call me every time, I had a exam. All say, that love do wonders.

"Dil to pehle hi mom tha

Tere aane ki aahat bhar se hi ye pighal gaya hai fir se".

I had for him the same love that lay suppressed in a corner of my heart.

"Please, don't leave me alone, now, ever, *beta*." I said.

"Love you, please don't say that. I am with you to be your and yours alone." he said.

"Promise? I asked."

"Yes, always and forever." he assured.

"Thanks, I will study now in peace."

"Who else would otherwise be a topper without your love and the right to love you again?" I said.

"He was proud of me and I was happy making him proud."

His good luck, before exams had done wonders.

"Another thing, I have turned to love him now with more of determined heart, but as delicate as the petals of soft flowers."

"Once he had told me that dad had asked his brother-in-law to speak to him about *haldiwali* (the girl his family had found for his marriage). If Meethu says no to dad, he will be in hospital. So he has to be ready with 4-5 lacs again to spend for his medical care."

"I am doing everything for them. They don't see my happiness. I am just thinking of their happiness all the time." He told me.

"You owe to do everything for them. They are family." I replied.

"If papa is not calling, you take initiative. If you had liked the girl, go ahead. What's the problem?", I guided him.

"He was mine and now I could love him the best way, I had always in my mind about loving him."

To him, "I never pour out my heart." Many things lay buried in my dwarf heart because he was alone and for me he was only companion for this life, too."

During exams, everything went more strong and it beautified normal beings between us. We were so happy.

Exchanging pictures that I had never thought of sharing with anyone.

"I had no day passed without his presence on my mind. Exchanging our talks, he was my pg (pati g) now, I had given my everything to him. Without him, I preferred dying, because it would not have been living.

Kuch ankahe shabd

Jab zehan mein utar jaate hain

Jo na jaane uske liye kuch nahi, jo jane

Usko sehlaab mein bha jaate hain

I had to say this and that. *Mujhse jaldi se shaadi karlo. mujhe apke paas rehna hai.* Bahut pyar karna hai.

Every morning, I want to wake you up and put to sleep at night, feed you with food, I have especially cooked for you, sit next to you for prayers. I can sit and stare. When my eyes need recharge seeing you. I can earn my livelihood whole life with this love as my possession. The way I love you is contrary to the way I behave when someone else stares at me."

His every single picture had been in my custody. I had ended up every social circle. "I could wait for him day long. I have even joined a school, it was his wish to see me in a school. I gave up the idea of salary, my wishes and even the work as a receptionist, later I was introduced to in the school I had suffered a blow on my self-respect. He was happy, I have nothing more to wish for."

I used to stand by the roadsides in such intense heat to talk to him. Speaking to him on phone and deciding and planning our future together was the best thing, that didn't let me bother sun smiling cruel at me.

I used to go then to MBA class and skip even the classes to speak to him again standing in stairs where there was heat and heat alone.

He had asked me once, *beta,* this gap, both of us, should not have, can you please?"

"Yes, I understand. What you mean to say here, but I will". I replied. He referred to the gap between front visible teeth, that was common to us.

Doctor had advised me not to go for this. You look good with this smile. It's been gifted by God to you. But I knew that only my God had demanded this from me, I told doctor, "I had to go for this treatment."

The first day she took the measurement and all and had given me a hint of how it would happen.

I felt giddy, because I never had such experience all my life. First 2-3 days had been the same, painful, but his only demand to rectify my looks appealed to me more than facing this pain.

For second session, she passed me over for an experiment to one of his juniors. I went unconscious, it hit my lower teeth like a grinding machine, I had so much pain when I opened to find myself alive.

I could hardly open my mouth and had cotton tossed in mouth.

'I had injected the painkiller, you will feel better for tonight, come back tomorrow.' the doctor said.

Reached home, finding mom with all slips of how, I had spent for treatment.

They don't pay, still they hold right to ask. I could not stand the sight of this and had ran to cry and cry with pain alone.

When I had given missed call on his phone, he had rang immediately. I had told him something that may not hurt him. But I was now hurt both physically and mentally. It had nothing to do with my being educated.

Only the doctor had behaved wicked.

I had not paid much of attention to my studies but to loving him. I had no interest about anything but in him and his happiness.

He used to get angry when I didn't forward him the demanded pictures on time. I had people around here and who used to think of what my smile was meant for.

His beautiful smile had let me smile, too, all the time. He would say something naughty like, I will throw you out of bed. I had always a hidden meaning beneath, I loved such messages. He had touched my heart with his pranks.

I wonder if someone had ever shared love being at Internet cafe, we did. It terrified me finding everyone present there, but really to share and do love this way. Being an educated, it had my love for him and had made me do things I had never imagined of. Love was the driving force.

"Love is never blind but sometimes
it closes eyes to things in love."

He couldn't pass a day without me and I, too, had a day wasted when not able to speak to him.

All the days are not same. Once he had trouble because of a client at Subway, but what was the problem with that being had remained a matter of surprise. Because after logging the complaint in, he had never turned up.

I had as per his instructions once been to see his dad. He looked healthy by now. Without anything in my mind, I had discussed with him about the smoking as I, too, had seen people spoiling their precious life because of it, the time I had worked with an NGO. I had no idea that I may hurt him with my request, but I was thinking of their well being only.

Later on for many days, I had seen him smoking outside the bank, he was working in. Why he is doing this, while all have loved him and requested him at times to leave smoking and to stay healthy for a life ahead.

Meethu was not in India. But I had all the time waited for him. He had once been with his friends somewhere, I had to see him on cam. But his message had baffled me. Coming again to senses, It was just a trip and he had been doing all right.

I was at my aunt's place and he messaged me telling that he didn't enjoy missing me. It had raised my expectation for love from him.

His slightest pain had not let me had a wink of sleep at night. He had raised the bar of vista by respecting and accepting my love. If ever he had wished to see me bathing, I had not knocked back this, too. I had assured, we will bathe together, when with each other. Such was my faith that made him stand in the same row, next to my God. I dared everything.

Pertaining to God love was omnipresent.

He could frown but I was resolute to stay sure of his smiles. Sometimes he had chided me but I had paid more attention to the love rather to this momentary rebuke. I had avoided every discussion that could make him derange. I would exit from being played as discussant. All I had for him was comfort, love and care. I had felt a million times sorry for if he had ever felt hurt.

I had once seen his sisters standing outside my study centre.

What they were looking for? It confused me.

They had no idea of it though.

That day had ticklered me as never before. But I greeted them and had gone to attend my class and received his call and told him what had eventuated that evening.

His wish to come to India and to take me along as his legal wife had only consoled. Book a hotel, he had said once I will love you there, I could not rejoinder and later he felt sorry for saying this.

He would be coming in august now for marriage. I am his wife, he will not let down his wife ever. Who would have otherwise a right to have such intimate pictures in exchange. Days and night hopped, in august, the puja ceremony, for which he was supposed to come lay nullified. I had somehow preserved his honor, telling my parents– the odds and evens I could. I will wait for my life time to be with him and its just a matter of months, only a couple of those. I had cried but had not let him sense, how hurt I was. It wasn't unfair to wait but the wait should prove worth.

I knew I was extra talented to hold on to things but the thing that was awry was my art of suppressing my feelings to suffer alone by paying the cost for my love's soothe.

Epilogue 1

"How much does a man need?"

Waiting now oozed as a bad thing I was good at. Not knowing was but more grievous to settle account for.

"Every waiting day made me little dwarf

Every lonely day made me a pygmy

Every day the fake smile made me a mimic

Every jumble up less capable of holding this faith alone

Though heart ditto"

"To Be or not to Be"

If you don't understand anything, do ask. I wonder how this was the favourite of all the lines teachers use to orate. I took initiative asking my teacher, HIM, but..

It was my love, respect and concern for I had chosen to wait in silence. He had no one by his side. He was always in my heart but.

My phone beeped coruscating his name. It was a text message.

Gugu, I know you are missing me too much

Beta I am with you.

Just close your eyes

I am right next to you in bed

Loving you like there is no tomorrow.

I am not going to phone to say this. I am fed up of this... I was to continue reading, he rang.

My hands jiggled as my poor heart clinched by retrospection.

Get ready for a rape, my Gudia..

... I am coming day after tomorrow for a court marriage, love and kisses from your husband, was message left unread.......

It ended my wait, as he phoned to say ... forget me, please ....

Epilogue 1

And the very next day, I could not see him on Facebook. I could not call him. I could not forget him too. He blocked me everywhere.

The reason, just hurting his father's ego with my serene request -

To leave smoking. He felt, I did somethirg hugely wrong, being a stranger to my future family.....

Tears rolled down my eyes, in the arms of another man ... when I felt once the same love, after ages....

.... and it continued my search for love, having my love, HIM , in my mind....

All thirty men I met were shrewd , till I met him & changed my destiny ..... To love & live with him ... But being alone ....